between war and here

By Carolyn A. Surrick

Upper Green Publishing

ISBN: 978-0-615-52427-6

Designed by Marilyn Drea, Mac-In-Town Graphic Design Services
Published by Upper Green Publishing, LLC
Photographs by Burgess Blevins

Upper Green Publishing

www.uppergreenbooks.com

1730 Crownsville Road
Annapolis, MD 21401

Bless the fallen ones

And the rising ones

Contents

Preface

Irish, Michigan, The Sniper and Wasim

Between War and Here

Coda

Preface

I do not find them sad. The wounded warriors.

We play music in the lobby every Friday from 11:30 to 1:00. It looks like a hotel except everyone there is wounded or is related to someone who is wounded. It's a place where you can see two men standing at the front desk, side by side, one missing his right leg, and the other missing his left. A place where mothers, fathers, brothers and sisters come to care for their dear ones.

All the branches of the armed forces are represented there, and as one soldier said when I asked her rank, "There is no rank here. I was a captain before I was wounded, but now I am just a soldier."

It is not a place for the squeamish. It is not a place for people prone to self-pity. Or maybe it is. Spend a few hours there and you might find it impossible to complain about, well, anything.

These soldiers aren't necessarily noble or heroic. But they are moving forward, some on crutches, some in wheelchairs, some without fingers or hands. They do what soldiers do. They assess the situation and complete their task, and right now their task is healing. They look out for each other and they know that sometimes the hardest wounds to heal are the ones you can't see.

And to me they are beautiful.

The Warriors

Stumpy

He rolled up in his wheelchair, stopped and listened. When I finished my tune, I asked him if he would tell me what happened and he said it was fine, he didn't mind.

He was in the back of a truck and an EFP* came sailing in. He said it was lucky, if it hadn't taken off his leg it would have hit his CO's head. That would have been bad. His thigh was too big for a conventional tourniquet, so his CO ripped the sleeves out of his own shirt, took one sleeve and tied it around his leg above the knee and balled the other up, stuffing it into the stump. They drove to the nearest aid station like that. Twelve miles. He never lost consciousness. I was doing okay, he said, I was even joking with the nurses before they took me in for surgery.

But he was mad when he woke up because they hadn't even tried to re-attach his leg. They have eighteen hours to reattach a limb. He was mad for two days. He was mad until his CO came to visit and showed him a picture of what was left of his leg. Not much above the ankle. We laughed about how it would have looked, an ankle and foot, attached right below a knee. Stumpy, he said, they would have called me Stumpy.

Before he left, he had a lesson. Since he only had one leg, I placed a scarf behind the instrument to keep it from getting scratched by the wheelchair, balanced it on my toes, put the bow in his right hand and taught him how to pull it across the strings. It screeched and squawked, but it got better the more he played. As he rolled away, he looked back, and with the biggest smile on his face he said, "Ma'am, this was a once in a lifetime experience."

* Explosively formed projectile.

The Captain

After she graduated from high school
she had to choose –
West Point or Julliard.

She was wounded in Iraq
a spinal chord injury.
I don't care if I ever move my head from side to side, she said
I keep telling them, just make it so I can do this again.

She closed her eyes, tilted her head, tucked her chin,
her left hand rose, fingers resting on the absent finger board
her right hand in the air, holding an imagined bow.

Blue Eye

Right after he was blown up
By right after
I mean when I saw him for the first time.

He was very still.
Quiet.
Blankets covered his wheelchair-bound legs
One completely blue eyeball on a half-scarred Asian face.
His head did not turn toward the music.
He stared straight ahead.

I never saw family visiting.
Never saw him talking with other soldiers.
I did not believe that he would walk again.

First on crutches, then limping, now striding.
He moves with fierce determination
His eye focused on the world in front of him.

Day One

Here's the timeline:
A few weeks ago he was in Afghanistan
Or Iraq
And he thought he knew what his future looked like
With X number of days left in Afghanistan
Or Iraq

He would go home for a while
Before being deployed again.

But then, something explodes
IED, EFP, rapid-fire Kalashnikovs.
Something explodes and things go really slowly
And there's a body part missing.
Or parts.

I try not to think about what happens next.
At least not explicitly.

He ends up here
For surgery
Or therapy, or prosthetics
And time goes really slowly.
Again.

Georgia Avenue

I saw a man lying unconscious on the sidewalk
he was not in uniform, but I knew he was a soldier

I ran toward him, people walked by
they walked around his body and down the street

as he opened his eyes
I put my hand on his shoulder
Don't get up. Just lie here for a minute
he said, No, I'm okay

Just rest, please. What happened?
do you remember what happened?
he shook his head and tried to stand up
I have to go. This isn't good, he said

Buddy, you need to rest here for a little while
did you fall? Did someone hit you?

he looked at me, looked straight through me
and then said

Sometimes when I think of the things
that happened over there —
tears come out of my eyes.

he tried to stand up
but his legs wouldn't hold

I stopped a stranger and she called 911
the medics arrived
reassuring, calm voices
they were so careful, so compassionate
as they cared for him I walked away

on that hot summer day in Washington DC
there was a soldier unconscious on the sidewalk
blood streaming from his eyes to the ground

In the House

Rule One

I never ask. "How are you?"
I say, "How's it going?"
It's either going okay or it's not.
But if I ask, "How are you?"
They have to tell me how they really are.

Not such a good idea.

Rule Two

You learn to assess injury quickly. In a glance you can see a gaping wound, a missing leg, a rebuilt face. Sometimes you have to look twice. Did they really replace his eyeball with one that is totally blue? Is he missing both legs and most of one arm? How can there be so many pins and screws in a shoulder?

No staring allowed.

Rule Three

It's important to make eye contact. If you can get a soldier to look you in the eye, and you smile, he might smile back. There are days when there isn't much to smile about and when you get to see one of those shy smiles from a twenty year-old, well, you just might start believing in god.

Rule Four

It's important to break eye contact. Some guys with PTSD vibrate at a different frequency than other people. You can feel their inner unsettled-ness. And they look at you, staring into your eyes as if they have something very important to say, but it is locked away somewhere so deep that it will never, ever be heard. So for those very long moments, their eyes hold yours, hoping you will be able to read, there on their corneas, the thing that is so very terrible that they may never sleep again.

Christmas

In December we ask,
"Do you want to hear Christmas music or Irish music?"
The answer is never Christmas music.

Christmas is about families
Being home for the holidays
Stockings hung by the fireplace.
The smell of cookies baking.

There are no children laughing
No stockings hanging
No cookies baking.

They want to hear Irish music.

Shoes

The mind wanders
Does he put the shoe on
Before he puts the leg on?

Families

She said
Have you noticed that babies don't cry here?
It's like they know.

Ghosts

A wife
Three daughters
She was thirty-five or forty
The girls five, eight, and eleven maybe.

Such sadness in their faces
Words whispered as they walked by.
Mom in front
Older girls next
The youngest trailing behind.

They walked by us four times.
We were playing harp and guitar and viola da gamba
A waltz, a hymn, a lament.

Their heads never turned.
We were five feet away from them
They did not hear us
Could not see us

In their grief, we were the ghosts.

The Nest

The baby was smiling
Happy as a bird
Sitting in the wheelchair
Snuggled perfectly
In the spot where his father's leg used to be.

Brave Mouse

Whenever a child walks by we play *Twinkle, Twinkle Little Star*. Then we change the words and do the alphabet song. The kids sing with us. Maybe not right away, but after nestling their heads into their mom's sweater, they peek out, and quietly join in.

I was playing alone and a little girl stopped and watched. She smiled at me and we sang together, then her mom called, "Come on, it's time to go. You are taking up too much of that nice lady's time."

The next time she walked by with her mom I asked her if she wanted to play. Her mom was worried that she would hurt the instrument but I told her that it would be fine. The little girl stood to my right and I placed the bow in her hand, cupped my hand over hers and we bowed the instrument together. She grinned as we played and then her mom said, "Come on honey, it's time to go."

I sat down to lunch near where they were sitting and the little girl came over. "Are you here to visit your daddy?" I asked, and she looked up at me and said, "My daddy got dead. We are going home today. My grandpa is coming to pick us up."

All the air left the room. It was not my place to cry.

His Father

I had an idea – what if *My Country 'Tis of Thee* could take the place of the chorale in Bach's *Jesu, Joy of Man's Desiring*? Ginger figured out how to make it work and now we play it every week. I don't know if the soldiers hear that the chorale tune has changed but the one time we played it in a concert, I cried.

It's the only piece I don't play from memory. It's complicated and I haven't had time to memorize it. One day I was reading the music off the floor and glanced up to see an older man walking out of the building carrying a leg over his shoulder, with a foot and a shoe. The leg was dressed in camouflage fatigues and in that split second of recognition I thought, "Oh my god, he's cut off someone's leg and he's carrying it out!" But he was pretty calm and there was no blood and by the time we finished the piece, I was laughing.

Their Son

Through the electric doors
Into the bright sunlight
They went with their son.

An embroidered eagle on the back of the wheelchair
My mom put it there, he said to a stranger.

I was eavesdropping as I walked past
I smiled and looked back
At his boyish embarrassment.

But there was little left of him
Both legs amputated high
and half of one arm gone.

His dad was quick to offer help
carrying the boxes and instruments.

Let me carry that for you.
Please, I can help.

Irish, Michigan, The Sniper, and Wasim

Irish

I

He said, "My mother is an angel."
Laughing, I said, "No woman is an angel."

He said, "No, my mother is an angel.
There were ten boys in my family
One was killed in action,
of the remaining nine, eight have purple hearts."

II

When his grandmother came over from Dublin
she got as many of his brothers together as she could
and when they were all sitting in the same room,
she said to them,
"My boys, you make fine soldiers.
But you've got to learn to duck."

III

We were comparing scars
Subcutaneous running stitches.

I have a titanium plate and twelve screws.
He has 1.3 pounds of metal in his body.
Not all titanium.
Different metals for different parts.

He was driving a truck when he got blown up.
Hands and feet were crushed.
Spinal chord injury,
Brain trauma.
Fine shrapnel in his kidney.

He's been here for six years.
Right before he was going to be released
They told him it was going to be another year.
His kidney was failing.
The screen they put in stopped working.
He could barely speak.

But they fixed it.
They grew more kidney cells
And healed his kidney with his own organic material.

He grew his hair longer.
He started complaining.
I asked a friend, "What's up?"
My friend said, "He must be happy.
You can tell when a soldier is happy because he's bitching about the army."

IV

He went home
to his wife and four kids.

His house has ramps now
and wheelchair-accessible everything.

Everyone is six years older
than they were the day he
walked out the door
to fight for freedom.

Michigan

I

his tee shirt said
Wounded Warrior
Some Assembly Required

both of his legs were blown off
one below the knee, the other mid-thigh

he sat in his wheelchair in the middle of the lobby, nodding off
a soldier stopped, tapped him on the shoulder,
"Hey buddy, do you want me to take you back to your room?"
his eyes opened, "No man, can't you hear it? It's beautiful.
The music is beautiful."
his hands silently conducted
then his eyes closed
his chin fell to his chest

another soldier stopped
tapped him on the shoulder
same question.
"No, he said, I'm good."
And he was.

In that opiated,
painless place
where music creates a world
without explosions and sniper fire,
he was good.

II

I'm gonna have surgery next week.
see, since they saved that part of my leg
(he points to part of a leg that has no bone, no muscle)
they can put in an artificial kneecap
and use cadaver tendons and muscles to build me a new knee.

I'll be able to walk again.
I'll have this one leg
well, half a leg
but half a leg is enough for a prosthetic leg
then I can walk with crutches.

They're gonna build me a leg!

III

No ma'am, I'm not from the city.
I grew up on a farm about two hours from Detroit.
It's quiet there.
Real quiet.

I can't wait to go back home.

The Sniper

I

What am I supposed to do now?

He is thirty-three years old and was a Special Forces sniper for fourteen years. The longest consecutive number of months that he was not in a combat zone in those fourteen years was four months. He was good at his job. Very good. Until he was blown up.

He was a right-eyed, left handed shooter. Now he is blind and deaf on his right side, walks with a cane, and can't bend his ring finger and little finger on his left hand.

They gave him a clerical job while he was recuperating. They told him where and when to show up. They never saw him. He was there all day but they never saw him. They never saw him because that was what his job used to be. He used to be invisible.

II

He said "Did you hear about what happened last year?
A shrink finished a session with some guy
Went up to the roof
And jumped off.

III

Major Nidal Malik Hasan (terrorist, psychiatrist, formerly stationed here)
13 dead
32 injured
45 people shot

IV

the day after Major Nidal Malik Hasan
opened fire at Fort Hood

my sniper's friends
sat right in front of me
while I played

they didn't usually
they might slow down
as they passed
but they wouldn't stop
and listen

but on this day
they couldn't find
their friend, my sniper

and by the time he walked
through the automatic glass doors
one of the friends was almost frantic
Where were you last night?
I looked everywhere.
I couldn't find you.
I looked for you until after midnight.

I went out, he said calmly
I went out for a couple of beers.

But I couldn't find you.
I looked for you everywhere
his eyes betrayed his panic

I took the metro and went to a pub.
What's the big deal?

his friend had reached his wits' end
You're a SNIPER, he almost yelled

As if that explained everything.

V

They stayed right in front of me while I played that day, the sixth of November, 2009. Their talk was crazy. Off the hook. Paranoid. Self-righteous. I had never heard them like that before.

When a buddy walked up on my sniper's blind side to bum a cigarette, and tapped him on the shoulder, I thought, someone is going to die today. My sniper raised his hand to do damage to whatever stranger had touched him, and his buddy held both his hands in the air and said, "Hey it's only me. I just wanted a cigarette!"

He said, looking his buddy in the eye, Don't Ever Do That Again and then rubbed his hands together to keep me from seeing them shake.

Wasim

I

Wasim.
It was a year before I learned his name.

This picture is burned in my mind.
A dark haired man in a wheelchair
Sunglasses hiding his eyes.
Sitting straight, proud.
Face expressionless.
Legs covered by a dark blue blanket.
Another dark haired man guiding the wheelchair
Younger maybe. Perhaps a brother.

The younger man shyly looks toward the musicians.
Slightly nods his head in greeting.
The man in the wheelchair
motionless.

II

A month later.

His brother wheels him toward us.
There are six of us playing that day,
The week before Christmas in 2008.

His voice is low, hard to hear
With an accent, but with perfect grammar
he says, "I want to thank you for coming here."

Under his dark glasses
A scar is barely visible
The blanket covers his legs.

"I love your music. It is beautiful."
He sits for few minutes
Then they disappear.

III

A year later.

I see him up on the balcony.
Walking with crutches
He waves.

I never thought,
never imagined
that he would walk.

Not in my wildest dreams
In all of the months
Of seeing them together.
His brother pushing the wheelchair
Wasim sitting tall.
I never imagined that I would see him
walking.

IV

I don't know when his brother came over.
But it was not at the beginning
of the thirty-five surgeries
and procedures
over seven years.

For much of that time
He was alone.

Thousands of miles
and across the ocean.
His brother came to help
change the bandages
count the pills
make sure they were taken with food.

Guide his wheelchair,
to appointments
to therapy
and back to their room.

It must have been hard
for your brother
when he had to leave you, I said.

There was a long pause –
He looked to the ground.
It was hard for me, he said quietly.

V

He holds degrees in math and physics
Speaks four languages
His father is a professor
All of his brothers and sisters have been to university.

He came to this country
and worked in a clothing store in New York City
until he joined the army in 1998.
Infantry.

He was wounded in 2003.

I asked if his brother would come to live in this country
No, my mother says losing one is enough
She would never let him come.

I asked him if he was going to go home now
Home to his family, his mother and father
Sisters and brothers.

I will go and visit
but this is my home.
I love this country, he said.
I am going to live the American dream.

Between War
And Here

Thanksgiving

The day after Thanksgiving
Air Force guy was
With his family.

Father, mother
Sister and her boyfriend
Brother and his girlfriend
Raucous and goofy
Together again.

I imagined that
Had it been eight years earlier
His sister's plight might have been
Relentless tickling.

Silliness reigned.
Pushing and shoving
Hilarity.
Almost as if on vacation.

But as they got ready to leave
Instead of
"I call the window."
His sister yelled,
"Okay, I get to push"
As she stood up and grabbed
The handles on the back of his wheelchair.

The Question, The Answer

The rest of the family went home
She stayed

When I saw them again
She walked
five steps behind his wheelchair

Wearing a huge white button
hanging from a string
around her neck

Its black letters said -

**I'M HIS
SISTER**

Between War and Here

She knew the date of his deployment.
His second deployment.
The first was Iraq.
Then Afganistan.

He hadn't been in country a month
when a Taliban bullet ripped through his leg.

He's the kind of guy who can lift a jeep.
Huge shoulders, powerful legs.
A quiet smile as he looked toward his wife.

She came to be with him
Leaving their baby with her folks
It's hard being gone this long, she said.
I miss the little guy so much.

They sat next to each other, listening
And when a tray fell in the dining room,
It spooked him. No one else heard it.

I saw him. She saw him.
Worry crossed her face.

He plays guitar, you know, she said to me.
Baby, why don't you go get your guitar?

He really could play
Focused, sweet, improvisation
Creating counter-melodies
Out of thin air.

The next week
I asked him if he had been practicing
Yes ma'am, he said.

He learned your whole CD, she said.

Track eight, he said, I love track eight.
I like the sad music the best.

After we had played for a while
she said, Play them your song
and he did

with all the heart in the universe
he sang.
His enormous arms cradled the guitar
Head bowed, eyes closed.
A rough, raw voice
A voice that has been there and back
Rang out.

His words, a lesson in
The distance between war and here.
The questions old friends ask
Who don't understand
What guns do
Who can't understand
What death looks like

They do not know
cannot know
What war sounds like
Smells like
Feels like
Is.

Withdrawal

He looked like hell a few weeks before he was discharged.
Is it your meds?
Yeah. They're trying to wean me off the painkillers.

They cut dosage in half starting Monday
But I fell asleep before I took my last pill
And when I woke up, I was shaking
and so sick
I couldn't keep any pills down.
I threw up for eight hours.

It's awful.
I can't play today.
Maybe next week.

That Boy Could Sing

The last Friday before he went home
we played track eight together.
And track two. And track nine.
We played a twelve bar blues in E.

Would you play your song again, please? I asked.

He sang it, Jesus, did he sing it
and when he finished
Air Force guy
(who had been sitting there while we played)
said, What the hell?
That was AMAZING.

In the pool this morning
I thought you were just some big clown —
Did you have to punch
me right in the chest?

A big grin crossed his face.
Thanks man, he said.
And I can punch you again,
right here, right now.
They laughed.

Christmas Eve, 2010

I said, Can I give you some music?

She was slight, frail
With a look of worry and sadness
That comes with motherhood.

My son loves music, she said.
He used to play everything.
Piano.
Trumpet.
Guitar.
He could play any instrument you handed him.

He can't anymore.
His arm. Because of his arm.

I saw a soldier on the other side of the lobby
in a wheelchair
Smiling at his daughter.
His father nearby.
They were happy.

She was not.

He wants to go shopping, she said.
It's Christmas Eve and he wants to go shopping.
And finally, now he can
But we don't have a car.
I should have rented a car,
But it's too late
And it seems like
it costs fifty dollars every time
We go anywhere in a cab.
We just can't afford it.
They would have given us a car,
But we didn't ask soon enough.

What am I supposed to do?

Her son turned towards us
His arm was gone, above the elbow.
But so were both of his legs.

Two Soldiers Walk into a Bar

It's lunchtime and we're in the cafeteria
A line forms as people wait to pay for their meals.

Two soldiers, side by side.
One in a wheelchair, missing a leg.
The other on crutches, one leg healing and one prosthetic.

The soldier in the wheelchair
Takes out his cane
and whacks his friend's prosthetic leg.

Hey! What are you doing? That's my good leg!

Devotion

She guided the wheelchair
Into the lunchroom
Every Friday.

Not much moved below her daughter's shoulders.
Sometimes fingers tapping, a little tapping.

They did not smile much.
Her mom would turn
And nod a brief hello
In our direction.

The daughter never did.

We saw them for months
And one day, the mom, distressed
sat down with us.

How are you? I asked.

I am so mad.
I'm not going to come anymore.
She doesn't treat anyone else like this.
She's nice to the doctors, to the nurses.
She's nice to everyone,
but she doesn't have one nice word to say to me.

It's hard for me to get here every week.
I bring her food, do her laundry.
I am DONE.

It was the last thing we expected to hear.

The Simple Things

Take a backpack off.
Put it on a stuffed chair.

Try to close a clasp
With one hand.

You have to hold the bottom part
Between your pinky and ring finger
And use your thumb and first fingers
(keeping it still with your palm)
To insert the tongue.

When your left hand rides useless
At the end of an arm
Permanently bent at the elbow
That's how it's done.

They Live and Die for Each Other

Hey! He yells as soon as he sees his friend.

The friend stands up and they crash knuckles
Only neither of them has any fingers.

It is the best the surgeons could do
With what was left.

They laugh and start punching each other
With their fingerless hands.

It's probably not only their hands
(Shrapnel goes a long way)
But that's all I can see.

They are warriors who were
taken away from the battlefield
Leaving their comrades behind
Their lives behind.

Now they are at the hospital
And no one wants to live here.

Not because they are afraid of pain
Or of being crippled.

But because the place they want to be
The place where they belong
is with their brothers.

In Iraq
Or Afganistan
Or Mogadishu.

They are warriors still.

Coda

The theory is: *We do what we can do*. As musicians, we practice every day. Why not practice in a place where it can change the world? Or at least change part of the world for warriors and their families. Music can be the cure for many things, from sleeplessness to sorrow. A harp can be a gift from heaven, a viola da gamba, the sound of a heart breaking.

I started calling in 2007, and in 2008 I decided I would not leave my perch beside the telephone until I had gotten permission to play for the soldiers. The Chaplains Office gave me the number for Peter Anderson, the director of our unusual hotel. When Peter said, "Sure, come and play on Friday," I'm not sure he imagined that we would be there weekly, for almost three years.

In the beginning I went alone, and then Sue Richards brought her Celtic harp, and Ginger Hildebrand her guitar and fiddle. We made friends with the patients and their families, the staff, and Pierre, the chef, who always had a smile and a hello for us (and made fine crab cakes and spectacular pastries!). The music was so soothing that the soldiers asked if we could come back at night to help them fall asleep. That wasn't possible, so we made them a CD.

I convinced Bob Dawson at Bias Studios, Charlie Pilzer at Airshow Mastering, Micah Solomon at Oasis CD Manufacturing, Marilyn Drea at Mac-In-Town Graphic Design, and photographer Burgess Blevins to donate their services and we recorded and produced *Above and Beyond*. In February of 2010, we started giving them away to soldiers and their families, and by the following November we had given away over 1400 CDs.

It is calm, beautiful music. Mothers find solace, soldiers find peace, and they sometimes find a place to go in their mind that is more about beauty than war. They say it helps and I believe them. When we do sell the CD we donate the money to the Special Operations Warriors Foundation.

I started speaking at the Rotary, at church, to my friends about our experiences with the wounded warriors and realized that I wished more people could know about this world of courage and determination. I wished that I had a book of postcards that I could show my friends and say, "there's Wasim, he's walking now!" or "that little girl was so sweet."

So here are my postcards.

The facility is closing down and by the time this book is out, our hotel will no longer exist. The staff is scattering to the four winds, some soldiers will go home, some to other hospitals, and where we will land, I do not know.

The days that I have spent with these men and women, and their families, have been extraordinary. Many, I will never see again. To all of them, I send my best wishes, and thanks.

A portion of the profit of these books will go to The Fisher House Foundation, an organization that donates "comfort homes" on the grounds of VA and military health centers so that families can come and be close to their wounded or sick warriors.

Carolyn Surrick
August 8, 2011

Author's Note

I grew up during the Vietnam War, my family split between the left and right. My brother marched in Washington against the war while my father was working at the White House. I never really knew a soldier until I met Dave Kanamine, who proudly served in the Army and whose father, brothers and sister served this country for decades. They have changed my life, as have the men, women, and children in these poems. Noble, honorable, funny, twisted, young and old, they are all dear to me. As is Bonni Lloyd, who reads, thinks, and then talks with me about what works and what does not, and Sara Kanamine, whose encouraging words kept me on course, and Amber George, who came into our family just in time to bring her red pen to bear in a most beautiful way. Thank you all.

Carolyn Surrick lives outside Annapolis, Maryland with her daughter, her beloved extended family, and two dogs. She received a BA in music from the University of California, Santa Cruz and an MA in musicology from George Washington University. Carolyn has been playing with Ensemble Galilei for more than twenty years. In that time the group has recorded eleven CDs, performed for tens of thousands of people in almost every state in this country, Canada, and Mexico, has done outreach in the schools with thousands of students, and has created four special projects including their most recent collaboration with the **Metropolitan Museum of Art**, *First Person: Seeing America*. She loves her work.

To find out more about Ensemble Galilei go to:
www.EGmusic.com

For more information about this book and the *Above and Beyond* CD go to: www.uppergreenbooks.com